Cosy Chill

Cute and Relaxing Colouring Book

Cherry Lam

This Book Belongs To

Before You Start Colouring

Welcome to Cherry's cosy calm world!

All you really need to get started and unlock the joy of colouring are your favourite crayons, pencils or markers.

This book has been printed on high-quality paper but as a precaution, we recommend placing a piece of card or thick paper behind the page you're colouring. This will protect the next colouring image.

We hope you enjoy the cosy vibes, cute characters and peaceful settings. Whether it's warm or cold where you are, take a deep breath and start to relax . . .

Happy Colouring!

Test Colour Page

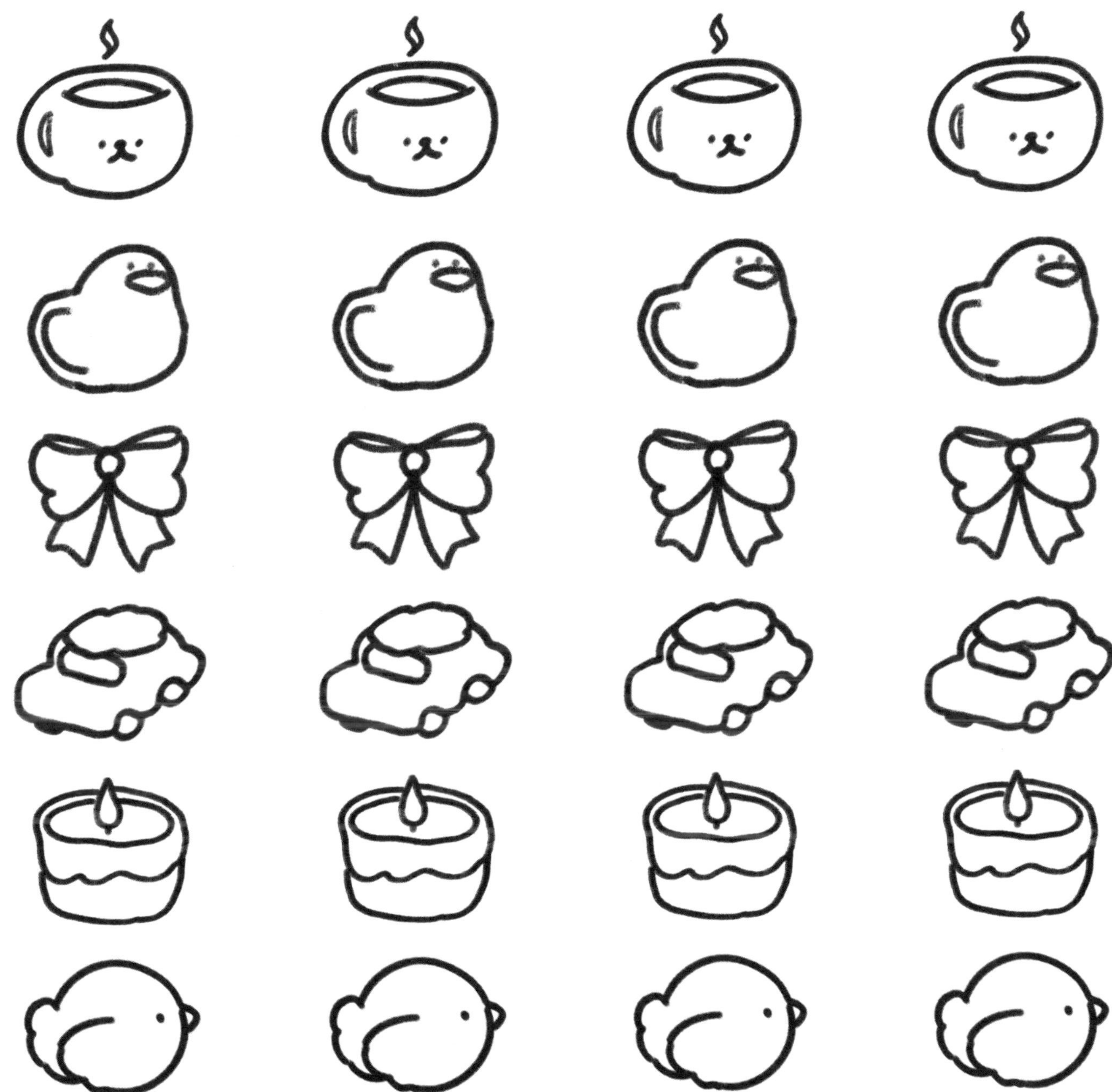

menu
$
$

1st
2nd
POTATO

latte
mocha
chai
matcha
BUTTER
バター
menu.

FROZEN
PEAS!

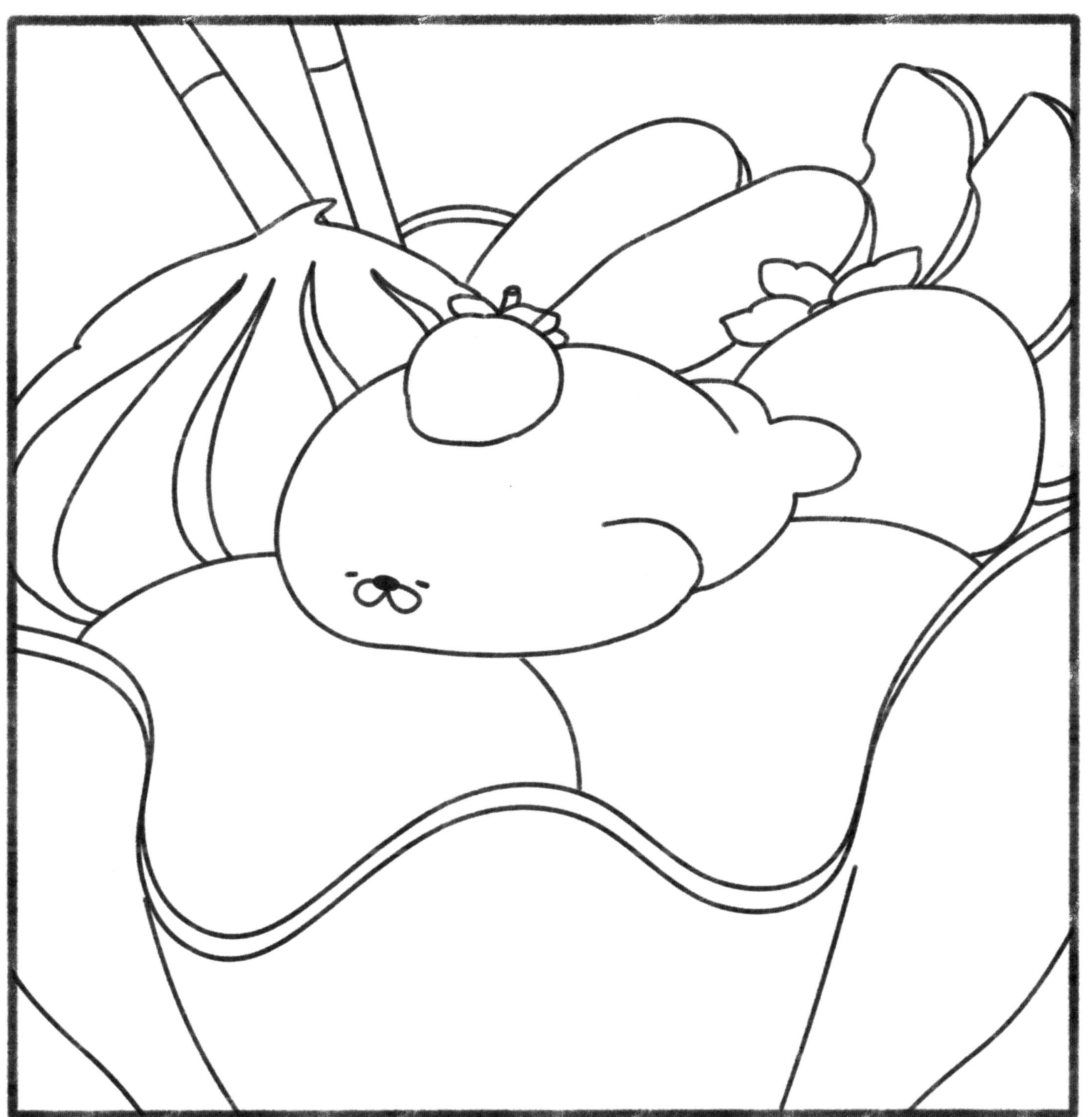

About The Illustrator

Cherry Lam is a self-taught digital artist who started her online art accounts during the Covid pandemic. Drawing with her touchscreen laptop, Cherry has accumulated fans worldwide through cute illustrations, comics of her original characters, merchandise designs as well as vlogs showing behind-the-scenes of running an online sticker shop. Cherry's Illustrations has attended many art markets locally in Brisbane, as well as in Melbourne and Sydney. Her merchandise such as sticker sheets, keychains, washi tapes and art prints can be found in many wholesale retailers, including in the United States, United Kingdom, Singapore and Australia. With a colouring book, Cherry's Illustrations hope to spread the joy of cute drawings by having people join in the fun of creating art.

cherrys.illustrations and **cherrys.art.gallery**

cherrysillustrations

cherrysillustrations

cherrysillustrations.com

PENGUIN BOOKS

UK | USA | Canada | Ireland | Australia
India | New Zealand | South Africa | China

Penguin Books is part of the Penguin Random House group of companies
whose addresses can be found at global.penguinrandomhouse.com

First published by Penguin Books in 2025

Cover illustration by Cherry Lam
Cover design by Adam Laszczuk © Penguin Random House Australia Pty Ltd
Illustrations by Cherry Lam
Internal design by Adam Laszczuk

Printed and bound in Australia by Griffin Press, an accredited
ISO AS/NZS 14001 Environmental Management Systems printer

A catalogue record for this book is available from the National Library of Australia

ISBN 978 1 76135 668 1

penguin.com.au

We at Penguin Random House Australia acknowledge that Aboriginal and Torres Strait Islander peoples are the Traditional Custodians and the first storytellers of the lands on which we live and work. We honour Aboriginal and Torres Strait Islander peoples' continuous connection to Country, waters, skies and communities. We celebrate Aboriginal and Torres Strait Islander stories, traditions and living cultures; and we pay our respects to Elders past and present.